A TALE OF TWO VILLAGES

Hedge End and Botley

by Bill Lyon

Produced by John Stranger
Published by Paul Cave Publications Ltd., 74 Bedford Place, Southampton.
Printed by Brown & Son (Ringwood) Ltd., Crowe Arch Lane, Ringwood, Hants.

Introduction

Time and space have a strange way of bringing the unlikely together, often several times. John Stranger hails from Guernsey and I am from Aberdeenshire. It would be difficult to begin further apart, however work brought us both to Southampton. In 1963 John became interested in Hospital Broadcasting, starting the musical output which was to be piped to hospitals in Southampton and Winchester. Ten years later I formed a committee which started Hospital Broadcasting on the Isle of Wight. I suppose it was natural that we should both invite Lord Mountbatten to open the studios. He also became the first President of both Hospital Broadcasting Associations.

Over the years as a Producer for the BBC I had quite a lot of contact with Southampton HBA and John Stranger but after I retired several years passed without us meeting again, until I walked into Hedge End post office one day to find that John had taken over as Postmaster. It was not long before John's enthusiasm for the area became infectious and he recruited me into the production of this book about Hedge End and Botley.

Coincidence again as this year is the 40th Anniversary of Southampton Hospital Broadcasting, and it sees the development of Hedge End's twinning with Comines in France.

Who would have thought that 'a strawberry field' would become entangled with Hospital Broadcasting, the Post Office, the BBC, industry, and an international development.

That is something for the next Domesday Book.

Bill Lyon

ISBN 0-86146-085-3

Published: December, 1992

Contents

Councillor
Peter Madsen
Mayor - 1992-1993

Foreword

As a life long resident of Bursledon I am very pleased to contribute the Foreword to this book depicting as it does the history and development of Hedge End and Botley. They differ much from each other, both having their own distinct identities, both important in their own way to the Borough of Eastleigh.

My first recollection of Hedge End is as a young boy who decided to follow an elder brother one evening to a fun fair at Hedge End — it was a long way for a very young boy who thought that the centre of Hedge End was just on the other side of Sundays Hill! A very tolerant father caught up with me at the fair in Upper Northam Road, and we all enjoyed what must have been one of the early carnival fairs following the Second World War. Hedge End was a very small village in those days.

My first recollection of Botley is an 'outing by coach', as a slightly older boy in the late 1940s, to a football pitch (now disappeared) situated at the rear of the 'Dolphin Hotel' to witness in an afternoon, one elder brother score a goal to help win the Pink Cup for a triumphant Bursledon Football Team, and another elder brother receive a medal as a member of a second triumphant Bursledon team — winning the Nicholson Cup.

Although there has been development in Botley, it has been done fairly discreetly. The Square has certainly changed in lay-out, and specialist establishments have encouraged and maintained business in the area. Botley also had some national fame due to the performances of local, national, and international jazz stars at the Dolphin Hotel. Bob Champion, a local 'character', who had so much to do with bringing international stars to the Dolphin during those times, still lives in the Square.

Hedge End is a much different story. There has been an enormous increase of housing, business, and shopping. Undoubtedly, the most significant shopping development has been the 'out of town' Marks and Spencer/Sainsbury development, and there are presently applications from them to enlarge still further. Local shops are understandably anxious at the effect on their trade, and this anxiety spreads to traders beyond just Hedge End.

The Borough Council cannot resist all planning applications, particularly, if they are part of greater overall Regional and County Plans. Indeed the growth of Hedge End is due to proposals of the South Hampshire Plan. The Borough can however ensure as far as possible that within the development good planning practices are adhered to, and adequate community facilities are provided. Many job opportunities have been provided, and apart from Crawley in Sussex, Eastleigh Borough has the lowest unemployment rate in the country.

The Borough is situated in a unique geographical position for transport communication, with access to road, rail, sea, and air. This is its advantage, and to some extent its disadvantage. The M27 to the east and west and the M3 to the north, the proximity of the ports of Southampton and Portsmouth, and railway communications to most parts of the country. (Electrification of the line between Eastleigh and Fareham in 1990 breathed new life into Botley station, and with local pressure and help from the Railway Development Society, a new station was opened at Shamblehurst Lane to serve Hedge End.) Finally, Southampton (Eastleigh) Airport presently being redeveloped already provides a comprehensive local and European service, and expansion of services are proposed with the introduction of services to other European cities. Continuing advances in technology will provide quieter aircraft requiring less runway.

Hedge End has acquired Town status, and generally the development has been handled well, with facilities keeping pace with increased population. Although there has been an increase in the population of Botley, it retains its rural village atmosphere.

It is difficult to visualise the future, but with the completion of development in the Shamblehurst Lane area, perhaps Hedge End will be left alone, although some community facility could be provided in places — for instance on land near the junction of Wildern Lane and Charles Watts Way. The 'Town' of Hedge End could have its own 'Town Mayor', and is presently about to twin with Comines in France. Hedge End and Botley may also find themselves in a different Parliamentary Constituency when the impending boundary changes take place. There could also be, in time, a different system of Council operation.

Whatever the future, I wish the residents of Hedge End and Botley well, and congratulate the writers of this book for providing information about two very interesting communities.

Councillor Peter Madsen
Mayor — 1992-1993

St. John's Church, Hedge End.

Below: Hedge End's first post office in Bursledon Road (now Hedge End Domestics).

A TALE OF TWO VILLAGES
Hedge End and Botley

Hedge End and Botley are two independent communities which come together under the umbrella of the Chamber of Trade. Both expanding, leaving behind the image of the intimate little village but at the same time striving to preserve their identities. Within living memory they have transformed from scattered houses along a dirt track road to middle class estates, industrial parks, motorways and hypermarkets encapsulated by a rather delicate green belt.

Less than 100 years ago under all this tarmac, brick and concrete lay the strawberry fields of Strawberry Village. It took the Second World War and a hint of progress to get rid of the strawberries in favour of people. Twentieth century Hedge End marks the centre of the Hampshire County Council Solent Development plan.

On the other hand 'Here are six ploughlands and eight villeins and four borderers with ploughlands, also a church, four servants, two mills worth 20 shillings and 12 acres of meadow." So reads the entry in the Domesday Book of Botley. It seems little changed today.

Botley has seen little development, where Hedge End has expanded from little more than a dot on the Borough map in 1870 to 1990 when it was second only to Eastleigh. The population increase for Botley is estimated around 400 from the period 1981 to 1994. For the same period in Hedge End, the estimate is between 5,000 to 6,000, mainly because Hedge End is identified in the South Hampshire Structure Plan as a strategic growth area.

On page 9: Aerial photograph of the centre of Hedge End prior to the development of the St. John's Shopping Centre – it includes the 'tin' church on the roundabout in the centre of the photograph. (Photograph by High Aspects Photography)

Hedge End — its origins

(As researched by Malcolm Butler)

The area that we now refer to as Hedge End was crossed by people 17 or 18 centuries ago, when the Romans, having conquered England, built roads in order to be able to move their soldiers swiftly in case of an uprising by the Britons. Evidence of the local Roman road can be seen along part of Heath House Lane. Travellers along that road at that time would have seen wild moorlands, heathland and woodland.

It is not for another 1,000 years, after the Romans, after the Angles and Saxons had conquered England, and after Wessex with its ancient capital of Winchester had come into prominence, that any mention is made of inhabitation of Hedge End as we know it. In the 13th century, 150 years after the Norman Conquest, a record had been made of land being cultivated in the Manor of Shamblehurst, and the name Adam de la Wildern was recorded. Later that century much of Hedge End came into the hands of Botley, when it became Common Land, poor wasteland unwanted by the landowners. This meant that the villagers of Botley could graze their animals there, and were free to collect firewood if they wished. This land was not owned by the local Lord of the Manor, descendant of the Norman conquerors, who, in the middle of the 13th century, was John de Botele.

The Kings of England also owned a great deal of land, partly for their own private hunting. The New Forest is an obvious example, but there was also an area right in present day Hedge End — King's Forest, which was later partly sold off and became known as The King's Coppice. This area finally disappeared altogether in 1864-65 to make way for enclosed fields and meadow. King's Copse School is a modern reminder of this old Royal land.

During late Tudor times, at the end of the 16th century, the first enclosure movement took place and sheep were grazed in many enclosed fields. It could well be that the first farms of Hedge End date from this time — Wildern Farm, for example. Apparently some original hand-made bricks suggest that a building was there about 400 years ago — now submerged under a new housing development. Heath House Farm (the house is still standing) is also mentioned in the middle of the 17th century, when John Mescott was granted the right to farm there. Hedge End Farm in Freegrounds Road can also be dated back to at least the middle of the 18th century.

By 1735 Hedge End was mentioned by name when James and Mary Lebburn became tenants of a cottage. They may well have been two of the earliest villagers and would have had their cottage either near Hedge End Farm or in Granada Road, close by the stream.

In a 1759 map of Southampton and district, Hedge End is marked and one must assume that a few cottages were here then as well as Hedge End Farm. Only rough tracks are shown, as no roads had been built then but the word 'cutt' is mentioned. This would refer to the focal point of the tracks intersecting in the area of the present village 'centre'.

1838 TITHE MAP OF "HEDGE END" [BOTLEY PARISH]

KEY TO HOUSE OCCUPIERS AND LANDOWNERS.

1 EDWARD TOMLINS – (JAMES WARNER)
2 GEORGE WHITE – OLD POOR HOUSE (PARISH)
3 WILLIAM ABRAHAMS – (PARISH)
4 MRS. FLEAK (OWNER)
5 WILLIAM DOWLING (OWNER)
6 WILLIAM ISAACS – (PARISH)
7 THOMAS NORRIS (OWNER)
8 JOSIAH ABRAHAM (OWNER)
9 PHILLIP ABRAHAM (OWNER)
10 HENRY BARFOOT – (PHILLIP ABRAHAM)
11 JAMES WHITLOCK – (PHILLIP ABRAHAM)
12 WILLIAM WELLSTEAD + JOSEPH WOODFORD – (JAMES TERRY)
13 WILLIAM WELLSTEAD + THOMAS OTHEN – (MRS. HAMMERTON) (THE OLD THATCH COTTAGE)
14 JAMES PHILLIPS (OWNER)
15 HENRY DUNDEE (OWNER)
16 WILLIAM DUNDEE (OWNER)
17 JAMES DUNDEE – (JAMES WARNER)
18 WIDOW TOMLINS – (OWNER)
19 JOSEPH LANE – (OWNER)

FIELDS A – K ALL OWNED BY JAMES BUDD.
L OWNED BY JAMES WARNER

TO SO'TON
TO BOTLEY
C. COMMON MEADOW
THE COPPICE (WOODLAND) D.
A. ABRAHAMS CLOSE (ARABLE)
B. COPSE CLOSE (ARABLE)
E. GULLEY MEAD (MEADOW)
F. HOB LAND FIELD (ARABLE)
PADDOCK (JAMES BUDD)
LONG CLOSE (ARABLE)
HEDGE END FARM (JAMES BUDD)
H. BARN CLOSE
LITTLE MEAD (MEADOW) I.
J. THE FIVE ACRES (ARABLE)
K. GREAT CLOSE (ARABLE)
L. POND CLOSE (ARABLE)
TRACK TO BURSLEDON
BOTLEY COMMON (WASTE LAND)

By the turn of the 19th century a new road had been built, running from Northam Bridge via Hedge End to Botley. The toll bar was situated just past the five mile mark from Northam Bridge, between Hedge End and Botley and remained there for about 130 years.

Possible origins of names in the area are:

Shamblehurst — woody area with few tracks or paths;
Wildern — uncultivated and often uninhabited land;
Hedge End — the name originally given to the farm in Freegrounds Road. The 1802 map of new roads shows a hedge running along lower Northam Road and then into Bursledon Road. The farm was situated at the end of the Hedge. However, at one time the village was called Edge End.

Early Hedge Enders set up home mostly in mud-walled cottages at the bottom of Bursledon and Freegrounds roads, on Botley Common where the streams provided water. They would have grown whatever meagre vegetables were able to flourish on the Common Land, and working whenever possible for the local landowners. Their life was hard — working six days a week on the land as well as tending their own animals, a cow, hens, possibly a pig. Firewood had to be collected and clothing mostly made on a hand-powered spinning-wheel at home.

Not until the 1830s did the first school open in Hedge End, indicating a substantial rise in the population. Gradually, local shopkeepers started up — among them the baker, beerseller, and shoemaker. This period also saw the birth of the division between Hedge End and Botley. Many of the agricultural workers of Botley, under the thumb of the Lord of the Manor, moved to Hedge End to gain more freedom.

The Tithe Map of Hedge End for 1838 shows the number of houses, who lived in them and who owned them. At that time it was part of Botley Parish, almost without identity. With the growth of the population came the growth in the number of public houses in the village. The first one in the village was the old Wheatsheaf, built of brick in the late 1830s. It was not a pub as we would know it today, but more like one room in a house, having a few spirits and a couple of kegs of beer. The Wheatsheaf was run for many years by Thomas Jackson and his family, hence Upper Northam Road used to be known as Jackson's Road. Some time later, probably about the 1850s there was also the Cricketer's Arms in St. John's Road. It is now the vet's surgery.

The name — the Cricketer's Arms — suggests that cricket must have been played from about this time, on a nearby field or meadow, obviously what has become the present recreation ground. A third pub in the village was the Fountain Inn, which dates from the 1860s. The original Fountain Inn was built in Chapel Drove, around the corner from where it now stands. The building is now called by the name Firtree Cottage. The Barleycorn began life in the 1880s as a beerhouse owned by the Dacre family. They eventually gave up the pub to concentrate on their brick works in the village.

In 1874, the Parish Church of St. John was built at a cost of £3,600. It seated 250 people within its Swanage Stone walls. It is interesting to note that the first burial was Albert Houghton (aged 18 months), soon to be followed by Agnes Adams (aged four), George Dundee (aged three) and John Chalk (aged four). Before you get the impression that it was not a healthy place to live in, you must remember that this was in a period when scarlet fever, tuberculosis and pneumonia took a heavy toll on the young.

Kelly's Directory of 1875 refers to Hedge End as a hamlet — a mile and a half west of Botley — once again establishing Botley's importance.

The first post office was situated on Bursledon Road and opened in 1880. It was run by Mrs. Aliza Banchini.

The commercial interests of the village by the mid-1880s was very much market gardening. Strawberry Village had arrived. Apart from the strawberry and vegetable growers the other commercial interests in Hedge End in 1895 were:

George Adlam and Mr. Herritt — beer retailers, Barleycorn and Cricketer's Arms pubs; Charles Page — Wheatsheaf pub; Mr. White — Fountain Inn and farmer; Charles Barfoot — shoemaker; Essau Barfoot — Marine store dealer and builder; Mr. Campbell — building; Charles and Anne Davis — post office, drapery and grocers; Sarah Dew — laundress; Henry Gunman — toll-gate keeper; Caleb Hughes — wheelwright and undertaker; George Oxford — brickmaker; Joseph Smart — brickmaker; Emily Wild — dressmaker; George Wild — blacksmith.

The main shop in the village was still run by John Terry, grocer, draper, baker and interestingly a dealer in the British Wines and agent for Blue Cross Ceylon Tea.

With the population growing there was a need for the presence of law and order in the village, so the first police station situated in the house next to the wool shop in Bursledon Road was set up around 1900. The first constable was Frank Hoare known as 'Squeaker' Hoare. Was this something to do with his boots?

Somewhere between then and now law and order slackened its grip. There is not a police station nor a resident policeman in Hedge End — the nearest being at West End. However, there is now a demand from many local inhabitants to re-establish a police presence in the area.

Today's development is a far cry from the beginning of the century when Frances 'granny' Allen was keeper of the toll-gate. She was only four foot six inches tall and sold small packets of sweets from the front room of the Toll-Bar House.

One sign of increasing prosperity in the village was the opening of the Union of London and Smith's Bank. This business operated from the front room of a house in St. John's Road, near the hairdresser.

Hedge End post office and Lloyds Bank today in the new St. John's Shopping Centre. Below: The Drummond Community Centre, built for the new development at Grange Park (Hedge End).

Nurse Gamman, a large woman, could be seen striding around the village visiting the sick. She lived in Bursledon Road and represented the only medical aid in the village. The nearest doctor was at Botley. Hedge End did not have a doctor's surgery until the Second World War, when Dr. Duffy set up at 86 St. John's Road in 1944. He came from the India Medical Service. Dr. Alfred Perm set up practice from 7 Winchester Street, Botley, succeeding his father. Dr. John Urmston arrived in Botley in 1954 and Dr. Watson built a small detached three-bedroom house at 26 Lower Northam Road in 1959; he then took on a junior partner, Dr. Robin Marsh, on July 16, 1962. Dr. Marsh became senior partner in 1968 with patients numbering 4,500 compared with today's total of 13,500.

Major expansion of the surgery started in 1988 when the partnership acquired the house next door (number 24) from Mr. Jackson, combining the two buildings into the present surgery. There are now five doctors in the partnership — Dr. Marsh, Dr. Peter Brewer, Dr. James Sibley, Dr. John Ponsford, and Dr. John Bush. The practice also includes three practice nurses, two health visitors, a health visitor's assistant, two community midwives, four community nurses and a psychiatric nurse. There are many additional services and clinics within the scope of the practice, including family planning, child care, immunisation, blood pressure clinic, diabetic and wart clinics and the Well Woman covering breast examination, weight counselling and cervical smear tests. Altogether it is an extremely busy and comprehensive medical service.

The Second World War brought about great improvement in the roads around Hedge End and Botley to facilitate troop and transport movement.

Looking back to the early days, poaching would have been extremely difficult during the winter months, as quite a lot of the land in the Freegrounds area would be virtually under water. The streams running down Butts Road and Bursledon Road would often be overflowing as they meandered towards the Hamble at Botley. The top of Butts Road used to be known as Quag End, since it often resembled a quagmire during the winter months, and there used to be a pond on the corner of Church Lane. Butts Road was so-called because water-butts were sold from a house at the end of the road and only changed its name to the present-day Granada Road, due to pressure from the Post Office. Apparently there was a lot of confusion with letters being delivered to Butts Road in Sholing, a district of Southampton.

Unusually for an isolated rural village like Hedge End there were two French families living there in the early years of the 20th century — the Valois and the Benoits. Henri Valois came to this area as a result of being a conscientious objector in France, seeking a quiet life in an out of the way place. He married a suffragette from Bournemouth, daughter of a well-to-do family. She is remembered for wearing trousers; this was extremely rare in those days. Trousers and a suffragette! Not exactly a recipe for obscurity. However, they set-up a business in Hedge End growing herbs, radishes and other salad crops under glass, with the wife seemingly doing all the work. She was known as a very kind and helpful woman. Her sister, Mrs. Sirnis, often came to the village causing some discomfort among the villagers as they could not only speak three languages but went skiing in the Alps. During the early 1920s they moved to Thornhill and Mr. Longster took over their land setting up his nurseries until he sold to a housing developer in the 1960s.

The other French family, the Benoits, or Tommy Benmore as he was called by villagers since they had difficulty with the French language, came from London. Louis Benoit was born in London as his father was an interpreter on the Cross Channel ferry train to Newhaven. Obviously travelling was in his blood since from 1898 he went on various ships, such as the *Orizaba* to Australia, the *Kinfauns Castle* to the Cape, and the *New York* on the North Atlantic run. During the First World War he was at Bramshott camp for Canadians, and after the war moved in with his parents who lived at Acacia at the bottom of Sunday Hill. Close by lived Lizzie Dacre at The Bays, just above Foord Road. She had worked at the Barleycorn Beerhouse for several years, helping her father run this and the brickworks. Lizzie and Louis became close friends. She nursed him for a short time when he was very ill with pneumonia. Her father then refused to allow her back into The Bays. So she and Louis married and moved into 'Belle Vue' in St. John's Road.

In 1929, Northam Road lost its obstruction with the removal of the Toll-Bar. The Mayor of Southampton, Councillor Pugh, was to perform the 'Opening' ceremony; but the night before some local lads removed the Toll-Bar. The Lances Hill Toll-Gate was borrowed for the ceremony and the keeper at Hedge End was kept busy by villagers wanting souvenir tickets of the last day. Part of the stolen toll-gate was found in the Recreation Ground and the toll-bar was kept until recently in the garage of a house in St. John's Road.

As recently as 1940 50 per cent of the marriages in Hedge End were couples both living in the village; so many villagers were related to each other in some way. With the development of land from 1960 onwards the population has taken small town proportions. The old families still remain but are situated around the centre, while large housing estates spread out where once were farms and strawberry fields, forming a typical middle class commuter belt.

I mentioned the centre, but there is no true centre of Hedge End. There is a roundabout at the junction of Upper and Lower Northam roads, St. John's Road and Wildern Lane. Spread out from this roundabout are the shops, thus creating a hotch potch of traffic and people. A recipe for disaster. When the new shops of St. John's Centre were built there was an opportunity to create a centre with a pedestrian way keeping the traffic and people apart. An area which could have become the true focal point of Hedge End was another opportunity lost through lack of vision.

Why the shops were not built to face into what has become the car park and so form a central square is a mystery to me?

The Old School

(From The Changing Face of Hedge End, *by Joyce B. Blyth)*

A piece of land at the fork of Bursledon Road and what is now St. John's Road was granted by Mr. William Warner to the Minister and Churchwardens of Botley by a deed dated October 17, 1863, as the site for the building of a school. Some of the pupils would come from the Ecclesiastical Parish of West End as they lived nearer the new school. On the foundation stone can be seen the inscription 'Feed My Lambs'. The school, until recently St. John's County Infant School, was opened as the 'National School — Incorporated National Society for Promoting the Education of the Poor, in the Principles of the Established Church'.

A grant from the National Society of £25 was received towards building the school and house. The remainder of the costs were defrayed by subscriptions and a Government grant. The running costs were met by Betton's Charity, and a grant assessed after Her Majesty's Inspectors had visited the school each year. If the standard of education fell, so did the grant.

The Sunday school teacher, Miss Permain, was appointed first headteacher at a salary of £25 a year, with a £5 increase the second year, if the managers were satisfied with her work. The first 13 children were admitted on January 18, 1864. Fees were calculated on a means tested basis. But from August 31, 1891 fees were abolished as the school took advantage of a grant obtainable under the Free Education Act.

By May 1, 1885 the building had been enlarged twice. Once with the addition of a gallery for the infants. The upkeep of the school meant hard work and many headaches for those who had the children's interests at heart, but many subscribers were willing to make an extra donation when necessary. With the aid of a government grant and many enthusiastic adults, an evening school was started in 1868. By 1892, technical education classes were provided under the auspices of the County Council.

Coming up to date, there is now a chance of visiting the school which has been converted into the Community Centre and Youth Club. There is a coffee bar open Monday, Tuesday and Wednesday from 10 a.m. to 2 p.m.; Thursday from 10 a.m. to 1 p.m. and Friday from 10 a.m. until noon. The Gym Tots meet on Monday and Tuesday mornings, the Youth Club on Tuesday and Thursday evenings. The Red Cross meet on Tuesday afternoons, the Disabled Artist Group on Monday afternoons, with Callanetics on Monday, Tuesday and Thursday evenings, Mind Group on Thursday from 10 a.m. to 3 p.m. and the Music and Dance for three to five-year-olds on Friday from 1 p.m. to 1.45 p.m.

On top of these activities there are various private parties, events, and social evenings; keeping this old building very much in the centre of village life.

The Old School, Hedge End which is now the Youth and Community Centre, situated at the junction of St. John's Road and Bursledon Road. Not everybody knows that you can get tea, coffee and snacks in the morning at the Community Centre.

Wildern School

Wildern School today has over 1,600 pupils and is the largest school in Hampshire. First formed in 1933, it was built on the site of a school since the mid-18th century. It took children from 'Edge End' as it was called and from West End.

Hedge End was granted legal status in 1894 and elected its own Parish Council who then set about developing education in the area. It is interesting to note in passing that at one time Hedge End was to be called Rosemary Hill. I cannot discover why. When the new school was opened Mr. H. S. Shelley was appointed the first Headmaster. He was to become the only male member of staff throughout the Second World War. He retired at the end of the war and was replaced by Mr. Simmons. A new larger school was planned and work on building started in May 1960. The finished building was officially opened by Lord Ashburton, Lord Lieutenant of Hampshire on September 19th 1963. The school was divided into four 'houses' but contrary to popular belief they were not named after strawberry types. The *Duke* of *Bedford* once owned the land nearby which he rented to Joseph *Paxton* who developed the Royal *Sovereign* strawberry.

In 1971 the School became known as Wildern Comprehensive School and that year also purchased a second mini-bus making it possible for greater numbers of pupils to be taken out on trips. The new art block was completed

Continued on page 20

Hedge End Station

During the century and a half that it has served the local community, the railway line which strikes south-east from what was at first called Bishopstoke Junction has been the victim, or beneficiary, of more unexpected twists of fortune than almost any other in Wessex.

The electrification and the recent opening on May 14, 1990 of a brand new station at Hedge End by the Minister of Transport, the Rt. Hon. Cecil Parkinson, MP, and BR Chairman, Bob Reid, inaugurated a bright new era for one of Hampshire's oldest railways. The line was originally opened on November 29, 1841.

Over 100 years ago the London and South Western Railway Company looked at a scheme put forward by locals for building a station called Shamblehurst, more or less where Hedge End station now stands. At an estimated cost of £3,129 this was considered in 1883 to be too expensive. Making allowances for inflation £750,000 has proved somewhat pricier. He who hesitates . . . !

This cost was borne by Hedge End North Developers and BR with a contribution from Hampshire County Council. Prior to the new opening at Hedge End, Botley was the nearest station and was itself modernised in 1990. During the days of 'Strawberry Village' Botley Station was used as the early morning collection point for the fruit going to Smithfield Market. Also the train carrying stone from the west country to Fosters Yeoman's Tarmac Plant ended its journey at Botley. At the time the new station was opened the Eastleigh/ Portsmouth line was electrified allowing Hedge End to be linked directly with Waterloo by fast electric train services.

Below: Hedge End Recreation Ground today.

Opening of the Hedge End Railway Station – May, 1990. Below: the new station.

Wildern School *Continued from page 17*

The 1970 Senior and Junior Basketball teams of the Wildern School.

The Wildern School Intermediate Netball team (1970).

This picture includes: Judith Dillon, Beverley Fraser (now Bryant), Anne Hodkinson, Norma Jones (now Perks) and Angela Case.

and opened in 1974, continuing the great development which went on throughout the 1970s.

In 1976 the head of the Lower School, Mr. Owen retired. As a final gesture he walked the Pennine Way raising a large sum of money for the swimming pool project. He was replaced by Mr. Durnell. The swimming pool opened in 1979. In 1977 the school suffered a great deal of vandalism culminating in an explosion in the biology laboratory caused by a gas tap being left on. The present Headmaster is Mr. K. Rockett.

Hedge End Carnival

The Carnival was first held to pay Nurse Gammon — the local community nurse — as she was not at that time paid by the State. Carnival funds were also used for many other community benefits. They provided an ambulance keeping it in service and driven by Nurse Morgan's husband until the National Health Service was formed.

During the war no proper carnival was held — a sort of fete was held instead. When the 'boys' from Hedge End returned from the war they were all given £5 from the funds raised by these fetes. Other beneficiaries were The Village Hall, The Day Centre, Hedge End Youth and Community Association, The Drummond Centre, two lanes were provided for the Bowling Club and an indoor Swimming Pool at Wildern School. Over several years donations were given to the Sea Scouts canoe store, £1,000 for a Children's Library, Kimber House and the local Guides were not forgotten.

After the Village Hall was built the Carnival continued to give donations to help with the running costs.

The present Chairman is Mrs. Greta Hindmarch who is following her father Fred Allen who was Chairman for many years. W. H. Abraham was also Chairman of the Carnival Committee. He was Vera Blunt's grandfather and he and Greta Hindmarch's mother were brother and sister demonstrating the close family ties throughout the village at that time.

There used to be a live pit in the Carnival with 'Bowling for the Pig' which carried on until late at night using car headlights. Fancy Dress was an important feature and the Carnival was held on the Recreation Ground with a fair run by Mr. Bartlett living in a tent before the days of fairground caravans. Mrs. Hales who died recently, ran the spinner until about five or six years ago. Senior Citizens of the village were given a supper each year in October. This year it was decided to change the supper to lunch instead.

The number of vehicles decorated to a very high standard and the other members of the procession brings the village to a standstill. Every July the crowd of supporters seems to get bigger and bigger.

Overleaf are photographs of the Carnival in recent years.

The Carnival . . .

Carnival day is a family occasion for which everything (including the traffic) stops.

BROADOAK BROWNIES

BUILT BY
ROGERS
& FRIENDS
FROM
SOUTHAMPTON

Hedge End W.I.

Hedge End Women's Institute representatives watching the planting of a tree presented by the W.I. outside the New Village Hall.

Hedge End W.I. was formed in June, 1956 with a yearly subscription of three shillings and sixpence. The first President was Mrs. Violet Haines, of Goodalls Farm, now part of the Heron Estate. Not many women went out to work in those days so the W.I. was well attended with many members learning country crafts.

The Jam and Jerusalem image has disappeared and the voice of the Women's Institute is now heard covering major issues nationally. Members now meet at the Hedge End Day Centre. Subscriptions are at £10.50 level.

Sadly, Botley W.I. ceased last year after many years existence — but hopefully is now re-forming.

Bursledon Windmill

This is the only working windmill in Hampshire and while not strictly in Hedge End it is within easy walking distance by taking St. John's Road from Hedge End post office car park, to the top crossing over the M27 on the way. Turn left at the T-junction towards Windhover Roundabout then follow the road round the back of the pub called Windhover Manor into Windmill Lane. A short distance down the lane you will see the entrance on the right.

The first windmill on the site dating from 1766/67 was replaced in 1813/14 by Mrs. Phoebe Langtry. It is her construction which has been so lovingly restored. This mill stopped working in the late 1880s.

Restoration work began in 1978 under the supervision of Hampshire Buildings Preservation Trust. It is now open to the public from May to September, Friday and Saturday and October to April, Wednesday and Thursday from 10am to 4pm.

How did the roads get their names?

It is also fascinating to look into the background of the many names given to the streets and roads around the area.

CHARLES WATTS WAY	—	Charles Watts was a former Hedge End character and Parish Councillor.
UPPER AND LOWER NORTHAM ROAD	—	Originally Bridge Road opened in 1799 by Northam Bridge and Roads Company as a toll road.
MOUNSELL WAY, LOCKE ROAD, RADLEY ROAD, DRUMMOND ROAD, STIRLING ROAD, WALKER ROAD	—	All names of former railway engineers associated with Eastleigh.
DOWDS CLOSE	—	Named after Dowds Farm.
PUDBROOK GARDENS	—	Named after Pudbrook Lake and Stream at Botley.
WILDERN LANE	—	From Wildern the ancient name of Hedge End area around 1700s.
SHAMBLEHURST LANE	—	Was also an ancient name for Hedge End area around the 1700s.
FREEGROUNDS ROAD	—	Named after Freegrounds Farm in Hedge End.
ST. JOHNS ROAD	—	Formerly Church Road but renamed with St. Johns Church.
ALLEN ROAD	—	Mr. F. Allen, at one time a councillor.
ALLOTMENT ROAD	—	At one time allotments either side of road.
BADER CLOSE	—	Group Captain Sir Douglas Bader, C.B.E., D.S.O., D.F.C., the legless fighter pilot — hero of Second World War.
CEDAR CLOSE	—	Cedars felled to make way for shops.
CHAPEL DROVE	—	Either side of 'Fountain' — originally a through road by the side of the old Bible Christian Chapel.
CHAPEL PATH	—	Next to Baptist Chapel — linking Upper Northam and Granada roads.
CHICHESTER CLOSE	—	Sir Francis Chichester, K.B.E. Winner of first single-handed transatlantic sailing race in 1960. Single-handed circumnavigation of world in 1967. Died August 26th 1972.

DAMEN CLOSE	—	Site of bungalow owned by Mrs. Damen.
FOORD ROAD	—	Mr. T. H. Foord, one time owner of Botleigh Grange.
GOODALL'S LANE	—	'Wildern', once farmed by Mr. Goodall.
HALES DRIVE	—	Site of Hales Bros. Horticultural Works.
HARRIS AVENUE	—	Air Vice-Marshal Jack 'Bomber' Harris, C.B., C.B.E. — World War Two hero. Died July 9th 1963.
HOBB LANE	—	Hobble — to tether horses.
KANES HILL	—	Netley Firs House, entrance Kanes Hill. Owned by Susannah Keans in 1844. Recorded as Susannah Keane in Hampshire Directory for 1859.
LAKE FARM CLOSE	—	Site of Lake Farm.
LEWRY CLOSE	—	Mr. C. H. Lewry, one time Churchwarden and Clerk to Hedge End Parish Council.
LONGCLOSE ROAD	—	Land of this name shown on tithe map.
MORGAN ROAD	—	Nurse Morgan, one time District Nurse. Twenty-one years in village.
NURSERY GROVE	—	At one time Longster's Nursery. Prior to that, owned by Mr. Valois.
OAKTREE CLOSE	—	Site of Old Poor House, with oak tree in the garden.
PARDOE CLOSE	—	Mr. Sydney Rimell Pardoe, was head gardener at Longster's Nursery.
PARK CLOSE	—	Was a cottage, strawberry and pasture land of this name.
PRETORIA ROAD	—	Dating from Boer War.
RAEBURN DRIVE	—	Name of Mr. W. H. Abraham's house. Dairyman.
RATCLIFFE ROAD	—	Mr. A. A. Ratcliffe, one time Headmaster of St. John's School. District Councillor and Magistrate.
RESERVOIR LANE	—	Contains site of old Reservoir.
ROSE CLOSE	—	Sir Alec (Richard) Rose. Single-handed circumnavigation of the world in 1968.
ROSEMARY GARDENS	—	Site of house named 'Rosemary'.

SIMMONS CLOSE	—	The late Mr. Wilfred Herbert Simmons, one time Parish Councillor. Served on Village Hall Committee.
SMITH GROVE	—	Mr. H. J. Smith, one time Clerk to Parish Council.
SOWDEN CLOSE	—	Mr. D. Sowden, one time Parish Councillor — Village Hall Committee.
SPEGGS WALK	—	Hedge End Farm, known as Speggs Farm. Botley Church Register 1605 to 1680 records Richard Spegg 'most ancient inhabitant'. A common name in Shamblehurst during 1600s.
TAPLIN DRIVE	—	Mr. Fred Taplin, at one time Parish Councillor.
UPPER NORTHAM ROAD	—	Village Centre to junction with Netley Firs Road; Upper Northam Close, from junction with Netley Firs Road to M27 underpass; Upper Northam Drive, from M27 underpass to Thornhill roundabout. Entire stretch opened in 1799 by Northam Bridge and Roads Co. as a toll road.
WATTS ROAD	—	The late Mr. W. Moses Watts, Parish and District Councillor.
WHEATSHEAF COURT	—	Site of 'Wheatsheaf' Beer House.

Overleaf: On the next two pages is an aerial photograph (taken by High Aspect Photography) of the magnificent super store of Marks and Spencer and Sainsbury at Hedge End.

MARKS & SPENCER
J. SAINSBURY

The Fountain Inn, St. John's Road, Hedge End snowed up in 1952.
Below: Fountain Inn darts team of the 1950s – including, Cook, J. Edwards, Merrit, Hawkins, A. Edwards.

The Footballers

Hedge End F.C. - Winners of the Pink Cup in 1935-36.

Hedge End F.C., 1956 - with all the cups they won.
The picture includes A. Smith, R. Sparshott, R. Maidment, H. Worsfold, P. Standley, B. Cutler, Merrit, I. Williams, C. Smith, S. Fell, R. Fell, J. Barfoot, S. Whitman, R. Young, Ross.

Botley Square today.

Below: Aerial picture of the Square and Winchester Road, showing Bugle Hotel (in the centre of the picture) one time celebrated stop for coach and horses.

Botley

History has treated Botley in a very different way. William Cobbett wrote: "Botley is the most delightful village in the world. It has everything in a village that I love, and none of the things that I hate. It is in a valley, the soil is rich, thickset with wood, the farms are small, the cottages neat, it has neither workhouse, nor barber, nor attorney, nor justice of the peace, and though last not least, it has no volunteers. Would I were poetical, I would write a poem on praise of Botley."

Cobbett came to live in Botley in 1804, living as a tenant in several farms including Fairthorne Grange and Raglington.

As mentioned earlier, Botley is listed in the Domesday Book, and is still a village with its square, market hall, flour mill, and Manor Farm Museum.

Manor Farm was owned by the Earl of Southampton in 1546, passing on to the ownership of the Duke of Beaufort in 1733. He then passed it on to the Duke of Portland in 1755. By 1831 it had come into the hands of James and William Warner, who formed the Botley and South Hampshire Farmers' Club. Hampshire County Council bought the land in 1978.

Botley is on the River Hamble — Hamble meaning crooked river — and is tidal as far as Botley. This makes it easily accessible. Several attempts were made by the Vikings to come up river. Shipyards grew up along the river with timber available on the densely forested banks.

In 1338, the first Royal Navy Man o' War, *St. George* was launched by Edward III. In 1346 the River Hamble supplied 18 ships and 325 men for the Royal Navy. This compares with five ships and 96 men from Portsmouth.

To cross the Hamble at Botley all traffic had to wait for low tide, then use the ford. Arriving at the wrong time could have meant a wait of six hours which might explain why Botley had 13 public houses!

Up to 1920, colliery boats came up the Hamble to unload. Some coal would inevitably fall into the river so it became a local occupation to dredge the river for coal.

Another local activity from time to time was a tug of war across the ford between the lads of Hedge End and the locals of Botley.

John of Botley who was Lord of the Manor and a relative of William of Wykeham, obtained a charter from King Henry III to hold a Fair and Market in the village. The market is still being held there and in the Botley Market House erected in 1848 are the preserved remains of an ancient oaken canoe from the time of the Britons. It is 13 foot six inches in length and was dug up at Fairthorne Manor in the autumn of 1888.

About 200 years ago Botley Mill was owned by a notorious speculator known as 'Kings Stares'. He brought widespread ruin into the neighbourhood with his unscrupulous dealings and died an untimely death in 1798 at the 'Catherine Wheel' now a local baker's shop.

Botley Station was a hive of industry during the days of the strawberries and Strawberry Village. Sixty horse drawn vans were needed to transport the fruit from Waterloo Station to the markets. Fifteen hundred tons of strawberries were grown during the last growing season in the district (pre-Second World War).

The Henry V Wreck

There is also an interesting wreck near Botley. It is all that remains of the *Grace Dieu,* now only visible at very low tides, lying where she sank after being struck by lightning and burning on 7th January 1439. The inventory for the ship indicated that she was rigged with one great mast, a mizen mast and two bowsprits, the longer upper bowsprit equipped with a large grapling iron to get to grips with the enemy.

The *Grace Dieu* was originally commissioned in 1417 by Henry V, about 125 to 135 feet in length of carvel construction. Her claim to fame was not what she did but for her size. In her day she was a Titanic. Henry V's foresight and development of the great British Navy was not carried on by his successor Henry VI. His savage economies rendered the British Navy impotent at sea and the *Grace Dieu* was towed from the builder's yard to the River Hamble — then known as the Bursledon River. Some years later she was moved to a site about one and a quarter miles upriver from the present Bursledon Road Bridge, in the Parish of Botley. She was the original *Grace Dieu* and later gave her name to the more historically famous vessel commissioned by the VIIIth Henry.

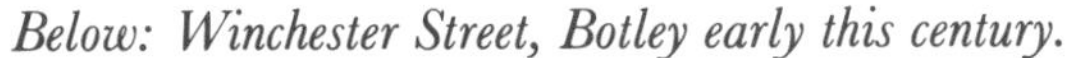

Below: Winchester Street, Botley early this century.

High Street and (below) Station Road early this century.

Overleaf is a photograph of the Botley Home Guard taken in 1940.

The Post Office

The Botley Postmen, 1914. The Post Office was gutted in 1940.

Botley Post Office also changed its site three times. It started on the same side of Botley Square as Lewry's butcher shop, then moved over to the opposite side where it was almost completely gutted by fire on January 19th 1940. Miss Ethel Maffey who still lives in Botley with her sister, spent a hectic time rushing to and fro with buckets of water during the efforts to bring the fire under control. The Post Office then moved back to a site which has now been incorporated into Circle K shop.

Ethel Maffey also paid tribute to Postman John King of Botley in her publication of April 1989. John King was born in 1860. He lived a very devout life and wrote many hymns. His 'In Time of War' was frequently sung during the First World War. It was his labours which kept the grass cut with a scythe at the Old Church in Botley. He was one of a family of 12 and became a familiar sight in the area on his tricycle delivering the mail. He died in 1923.

Botley Church and School

The original Mr. Lewry of Botley outside his butcher's shop in 1908.
Below: The Botley home of the great campaigner William Cobbett.

Above: Mr. Nick Hillier is the present owner of the business
Below: High Street today.

Above: The old Botley church, situated beside Botley Manor Farm.

Opposite: The clock on All Saints' (the new church at Botley) was originally on the turret of Cobbett's Stables.

The Churches of Botley

There were strong links between farming and the Church until modern times. The parson too was closely involved with farming. Not only did he receive payment of tithes — in cash or kind — but he also farmed the church glebeland. An area of woodland at Botley called Parson's Coppice owes its name to a dispute over tithes between the rector and a local landowner.

Rural families have worshipped on the site of the Old Church of Botley for over 900 years. A church was mentioned at the time of the Doomsday and stood near the line of the Roman road.

The present stone building built around 1282, continued as Botley Parish Church until 1836. The nave was damaged by a falling tree so had to be pulled down. The repairs reduced the church to half its size.

Botley had by this time been centred on its present main street and it was much more convenient for the village to have a new Anglican church in that area. The graveyard at the Old Church continued to be used occasionally until the last war. The old stones and the memorials commemorate many of the people who lived at Manor Farm. There are several elaborately carved 18th century stones, like that of Mary Wellstead, who died in 1767 apparently after a long and painful illness.

There is also the grave of Isaac Earwicker, whose home has been re-created at Manor Farm. He died in 1905 at the age of 74 and his wife Sarah was buried beside him ten years later. Isaac was for many years, the farm bailiff for Mr. Edmund Warner, who lived at nearby Steeple Court and inherited the Warner estates. Botley Old Church is one of the few churches in the country which has detailed records of the seating plans which were universal. The pews were each allocated to the owners or occupiers of particular properties in the district. The old hand-drawn hearse can be seen in perfect condition within the church.

The new church took the name All Saints, so the old Parish Church was re-dedicated St. Bartholomew the patron saint of bees.

The new church was built in Gothic style in 1835. In the south wall is the figure which was brought from the old church and thought to be John de Botteley. There are four bells, all from the old church — three cast about 1400. The clock was presented by John Jenkyns having been taken from the turret in Cobbett's Stables, Church Lane.

The normal font used for baptising today's village children probably came from the original church. It was found half buried in a nearby field in 1740. Padlock marks for a cover can still be seen and must have been made around 1236 when locks were enforced to prevent the misuse of holy water.

Botley School rounders' team of 1969.
Back Row: Denise Small, David Kinally, Fiona Martin, Stephen White.
Front Row: Ruth Fox, Philip Hill, Ian Bradbury, Jamie Griggs, Gill Pink

Botley Primary School.
Delia Pugh (Headteacher)

Back Row: James Hollidge, Carl Spanswick, Steven Allen, Justine Bartle, Haley Grinhan, Jennifer Gibbon, Helen Cheshere, Edward Bandey, Simon Dennis, Louisa Page.

Middle Row: Rachel Folks, Alex Davies, James Gibbon, Stuart Stamp, Amy Maddick, Matthew Rolfe, Carl Sherwood, Nicholas Hodges, Richard Harvey, Celine Machola, Matthew Woollard.

Front Row: Lewis Maxwell, Katie Matthews, Alison Duncan, Wayne Jones, Louise Davies, Christopher Hussey, Fiona Duncan.

Botley School

To give it its proper title Botley C.E. (Controlled) Primary School is situated in the centre of the village opposite All Saints Church.

The school has large grounds which are well maintained. To the front is the staff car park, a large playground with play markings and a front lawn with shrubs, a pond and flower borders. To the side of the school is a second play area marked for tennis, netball and cycling proficiency. Adjacent to this is the outdoor heated swimming pool, provided by the PTA in 1971. To the rear is a large grass area with a football pitch, three rounders pitches, sports lanes and two sandpits. The grounds contain oak trees protected by preservation orders. There is also a small well-used conservation area with three ponds.

Botley National School was opened on Tuesday, January 1st, 1856. The Head Teacher was Mr. Alfred Williams, his principal terms of engagement were to instruct both boys and girls in everything but needlework, a task to be undertaken by his wife. A house was supplied, free of rent and taxes and his annual salary was £60, plus a £6 allowance for coal, out of which the school fires were to be supplied.

Children were admitted to the school by the clergyman of the parish and no child under five years of age. Every child had to pay twopence per week, in advance every Monday morning. Children of parents above labouring classes had to pay fourpence a week. Children had to be sent to school clean and punctual.

The old school which was built in 1850 has recently been decorated and a new heating system installed. It now houses two classrooms, music/TV room, with toilet and wash areas. A new block was added to the site in 1967 and houses the Headteacher's office, administration office, main hall, three infant classrooms, one junior classroom, library, resource room, staff room, two stock rooms, two large walk-in cupboards, large kitchens and toilets. There is also a pre-fabricated building closeby with two classrooms. So you can see how greatly the little school of over 150 years ago has increased.

The present Headteacher is Mrs. Delia Pugh and her pupils come from far and near. Frequent requests for non-catchment placements are received reflecting the excellent reputation of the school.

Manor Farm Museum

Manor Farm and the Upper Hamble Country Park cover an area of 400 acres, comprising farmland and ancient woodland.

The Farm has a range of typical traditional farm buildings including stables, hen house, pig sties, granary, cart shelter, cowshed and milking stall, the Red Barn, Longstock Staddle Barn, Thatched Barn, wheelwright's shop and blacksmith's forge.

The Thatched Barn dates back to the 1500s while the Red Barn, dating from the late 1700s, is the finest building on the site.

Part of the Farm House is lived in today while the other half is open to the public depicting life about 100 years ago.

To reach the farm by car, leave the M27 at Junction 8 turning towards Hedge End and take the second turning on the right, Pylands Lane, sign-posted Upper Hamble Country Park.

Or you can walk up Bursledon Road from Hedge End Post Office car park, then turn left into Pyland's Lane. There is a public bridleway through the Park to Manor Farm Museum. There are many walks through the Park.

Manor Farm is a major educational resource in the county, providing first-hand knowledge of a vital industry and introducing young people to the ideas of conservation and management of the environment. It is visited each year by thousands of school children.

Special school activities are arranged for small groups of children from first and middle schools. They come in costume and carry out various tasks, working with animals on the farm and carrying out many household tasks from washing and blackleading to preparing lunch.

A programme of regular weekend events arranged in the summer for the family includes demonstrations of steam threshing, sheep dipping and shearing. The main seasonal festivals of the countryside are also celebrated e.g. May Day, Michaelmas Fair and a Christmas Carol Service with local schools. From time to time major events are held at the farm such as the Sheep Fair, Heavy Horse Day and Flower Show.

Junior Rangers meet monthly for activities in the woodlands and on the farm and are organised by the Park Ranger.

Volunteers are welcome to help with fund-raising and a wide variety of tasks about the farm. People with an interest in the woodlands, for example, make traditional products for sale, including rakes and stools.

Manor Farm Museum and (below) interior of the souvenir shop.

Botley Mills

According to the Domesday Book of 1087 there were two mills in Botley worth 20 shillings. However, nothing more was known of Botley Mills until 1307 when St. Elizabeth's College, Winchester took possession. The theory that monks operated the mill during the previous 250 years could be correct. Thomas Wriothesly who was Earl of Southampton then The Duke of Portland, owned the mill from 1536 until 1775. There is also an entry that Thomas Everad rented the mill consisting of 'two mills under one roof with stream for £15 per year'. The present main building together with the house, bolting mill, stables and hogstyes, was built around 1770.

The Rev. Richard Eyre became owner in 1775 and it remained in his family until James Warner bought it in 1833. Recently a stone was found bearing the inscription 'J.W. 1835'.

Warner, unlike his predecessors, only had control for a very short time, for in 1838 William and James Clarke bought it and the mill traded under the title W. and J. Clarke until 1921 when Botley Flour Milling Co. Ltd., was formed.

Although flour has been milled at Botley for many centuries the policy of the company was forward looking and with modernisation and up-to-date milling techniques has always kept abreast of the times.

Water power can still be used to drive the stones for speciality stoneground wheatmeal flour but more often electricity is used today.

The Animal Feed Mill has undergone similar changes. Rations in the early days of compounding were highly complex and mixed on the floor in meal form. It was not until 1954 that a cuber was introduced. Now a new major development has taken place with the installation of a competely new compounding plant giving vastly increased output and improved flexibility in the use of ingredients.

The new modern mill can be seen at the recently developed Hedge End Retail Park. The original mill at Botley is divided into small units making use of what would otherwise become derelict building. The tide still rises and ebbs under the road bridge, the stones still grind and if you can close your eyes to the cars and the recently added boxlike units under the arch you can transport your imagination back several hundred years. In spite of the modern additions it is still worth a visit.

Botley Mills. Below: Botley F.C. – Winners of South Hants Hospital Cup, 1921.

Botley Community Centre, which adjoins the Recreation Ground.

Grange Aviaries

Situated in Woodhouse Lane on the Hillier Garden Centre site, Grange Aviaries is a family controlled and operated firm specialising in the sale of livestock and associated equipment. Founded in 1973 it is one of the largest pet and aviary centres on the south coast. It is personally supervised by Mr. and Mrs. Bernard Rogers and managed by Martin McLellan.

Martin's brother, Neil, recognised the need to provide customers with expert advice and enrolled for the City and Guilds Pet Store Management course which he passed in June 1989. His thirst for knowledge has not stopped there. In a closely fought National Contest to find Pet Shop Assistant of the Year, Neil came second. He has now been appointed Manager of Grange Aquatics which specialises in the sale of coldwater and tropical fish and associated equipment. In spite of the fact that the main shop is laid out like a supermarket, Bernard and Beryl find that it invariably pays to make an approach to prospective customers. Unlike ordinary shoppers the majority of people seeking pet products require some form of expert guidance.

When asked why he chose Botley area for the shop Bernard told me the choice was obvious since it was convenient to both urban and rural areas and Hedge End was top of the County Planning list for great development. Being associated with a Garden Centre has allowed an area for displaying the greatest variety of birds and aviaries in a very attractive setting. The close proximity of the Coffee Shop and Garden Centre make for a pleasant afternoon's browsing.

Botley Volunteer Fire Brigade

In 1914, a Fire Appliance Committee was formed in Botley, and the arrival of the first horse-drawn fire engine on May 8, 1914, saw the institution of the Botley Volunteer Fire Brigade.

In 1929, Mr. Roxburgh, of Roxburgh and Scivier, was commissioned to build a new fire engine.

In 1935 Botley Volunteer Fire Brigade was called to a fire at the Fountain Inn, Hedge End. Their efforts were not successful as the building was completely burned down. The new Fountain Inn was built behind the old site.

After 24 years service the Botley Volunteer Fire Brigade discontinued with the coming of Air Raid Precautions and the passing of the Fire Brigade Act in 1938 when responsibility passed to Winchester Rural District Council.

Here is a list of the equipment sold to the Winchester Rural District Council on their taking over the brigade:

486 ft. good hose at 9d per ft.	£18 4s 6d
608 ft. fair hose at 6d per ft.	£15 4s 0d
15 pairs couplings at 10s per pair	£7 10s 0d
1 ladder hook (new)	£1 0s 0d
1 pair rubber gloves	2s 6d
1 screw stand pipe	£6 0s 0d
1 bayonet stand pipe	
1 dividing breeching	£1 10s 0d
3 branches and nozzles	£3 0s 0d
1 branch and spray	£1 0s 0d
2 nozzles	5s 0d
1 hydrant key and bar	5s 0d
1 adapter	5s 0d
1 truck	£3 0s 0d
5 buckets	2s 0d
2 hurricane lamps	2s 6d
1 preventor	2s 6d
1 electric hand lamp	12s 6d
1 extending ladder	£2 10s 0d
	£60 15s 6d

The motor trailer pump was also sold to the District Council at a later date for £5.

The horse-drawn engine had been previously sold to a private individual in 1938 for £3.

Opposite: This was the original Botley Fire Station (now a private house).

Below: Botley Fire Station today.

Fairthorne Manor

The first traces of occupation are from the Roman period. Pieces of tile have been found and the settlement may have been centred around a brick and tile works, for which the local clays are very suitable. A Roman bowl found embedded in the river bank in the 1960s has been identified as Samian ware from about AD 100. At low tide it would have been possible to ford the Hamble here and traces of a crossing place have been found near to the present site of Botley sewage farm.

The Roman road from Portchester and Wickham probably crossed the river here on its way through the old Botley village to Clausentium (Bitterne). After the Romans left, the site presumably fell into decay until the arrival of the Saxons. Thereafter, the original Botley village with its church was built just across the ford from Fairthorne. A font, thought to be of Saxon date, was found in the river bed in 1740; it can now be seen in All Saints' Church, Botley.

The estate remained in the hands of a group of related families for some 300 years. However, at some point in the early 17th century the manor came into the hands of the Wriothesley Earls of Southampton, Lords of Titchfield who had already acquired the manor of Botley.

William Cobbett, writer, reformer, political agitator, and Member of Parliament, took up residence in Botley in 1805. Among the many properties he purchased was the Fairthorne estate, then comprising some 300 acres. The legacy he left behind can be seen today in the many trees he so assiduously planted for his children. The great Californian Redwoods and the Canadian Maple on the main drive were almost certainly Cobbett's planting.

The arrival of the 19th century railway with its station at Botley led to the construction of a number of substantial country homes for wealthy town dwellers. One of these was Fairthorne.

Built in 1854, the house is one of the better local examples of Victorian architecture. It was built for Clement Milward, Q.C., Treasurer of the Middle Temple in London and a man of some standing. His monogram can be seen in the south wall of the house.

In 1878, the entire estate, except the part held by the Rev. Jenkyns, of Botleigh Grange, was sold for £52,000 to Robert Anthony Burrell and his sister, Augusta. The Burrells were from Durham, from a family of wealthy mine owners. Robert Burrell died in June 1910 at the age of 81. As a memorial to the brother, Augusta endowed the accident wing of the Royal South Hants Hospital, Southampton.

Just before Christmas 1923, Augusta Burrell fell on the stairs at Fairthorne and broke an ankle. Aged 84 and already upset by the death of her god-daughter, Edith, she did not recover, and died on April 25, 1924. She was buried beside her brother in Curdridge churchyard where two similar crosses mark their graves.

She left a trust fund, called the Burrell Trust, to provide coal for the poor of the parish, which nowadays provides hampers at Christmas.

In 1946, although it was offered in lots, the estate was then acquired as a complete unit by the Y.M.C.A. to accommodate T. S. *Warfleet,* at the price of £8,500. The purchase ensured that we are still able to see a complete estate and grounds. When *Warfleet* closed its doors, the National Council of Y.M.C.A. carried out a feasability study and evolved a development plan, the result of which can be seen today. For several years, work at Fairthorne continued. One of their first acquisitions was 'Jason', a cement lighter converted into a houseboat moored off the village of Hamble. Commissioned in 1965, it has since served as a base for instruction in small craft sailing. Four years later, in September 1969, the Drapers' Company of the City of London presented the Y.M.C.A. with a fine new boathouse to replace the old structure; this new boathouse was the largest all-wooden building of its kind and won a Civic Trust award for design in 1972.

In 1970, Rotary Clubs got together and created the Coffee Bar meeting room. Lt.-Col. V. A. J. Heald who did much to pioneer the modern Fairthorne gave his name to Heald House, opened in May 1974, by 'Round the World' yachtsman Sir Alec Rose.

Initially Fairthorne set out to teach youngsters to sail and canoe and live in harmony with one another. Since those early years, the range of activities has widened and children of all ages and nationalities can now take part in such activities as archery, horse-riding, canoeing, and sailing, football camps with trained coaches, field studies, obstacle and assault courses and expeditions, and a golf course.

A new venture in the late 1980s was the creation of a conservation and nature reserve in a six-acre ancient woodland known as Pinkmead Copse. The land was purchased in 1980, but not until 1988 was anything done with it. Following the Great Storm of 1987 much work was needed to clear and make safe trees which had suffered in the high winds. With the help of a £15,000 grant from Barclays Bank under their Youth Action Scheme, the copse is to be turned into an area of special interest with emphasis on accessibility to the disabled. Sailing, too, now caters for the physically handicapped, with specially adapted Drascombe Gig boats bought with the money from the Children in Need Appeal.

A new climbing tower has added another dimension outside the boathouse, funded by TVS.

In November 1988, to mark the close of its centenary year, St. Peter's Church gave a large wooden cross to replace one which had rotted away. This is now situated on the front wall of the manor.

There is an excellent booklet *Fairthorne – Past and Present,* available at the Manor. To discuss any of the courses organised by the centre, please contact the Director, Y.M.C.A. National Centre, Fairthorne Manor, Curdridge, Southampton, SO3 2GH or telephone Botley (0489) 785228.

T.S. Warfleet

by George Vince

I came to Fairthorne Manor in 1947 to open a Sea Training Centre. Fairthorne Manor became known as T.S. *Warfleet,* which had, pre-war, centred on Dartmouth, as a British Boys for British Yachts Centre, started by Vernon McAndrew, a well known shipping magnate interested in winning the America's Cup. He owned a 12 metre yacht called *Trivia.* Unfortunately Vernon McAndrew and his ship *Gallant Campeador* were lost through enemy action along with the ship's company. Consequently a scheme was set up between the trust and the YMCA to open Fairthorne Manor as a training ship for young lads hoping to go to sea in either the Royal or Merchant Navy or in yachts.

Initially the scheme was funded for 30 boys but as years progressed this number more than doubled. At least 30 per cent of the pupils were accepted as apprentices in the Merchant Navy. With progress, things developed at Fairthorne Manor and people were accepted for camping, canoeing and sailing.

In 1951 T.S. *Warfleet* was chosen to look after the Royal Dinghy which had been presented to HRH Prince Philip on his wedding day. This was a 14-foot RNSA dinghy built in New Zealand to be carried aboard any ship commanded by Prince Philip. The dinghy had a very full life and is still in being. It was never beaten in class including ten years at Cowes Week.

During its period as a training ship, Fairthorne Manor was run exactly as a ship with watches day and night and a complete centre organised as any other nautical establishment.

Fairthorne Manor has for many years been known for its daffodils — one of the sights to see in the grounds in Spring.

Over the 13 years I was there it developed more and more with outdoor activities to become the Outdoor Activity Centre you can see today. For me the situation could not be improved with its grounds, river and access to the Solent. Hundreds of youngsters went through Fairthorne Manor every week, some of whom keep in regular touch with me. There is no doubt that the establishment has done great work since being associated with the Y.M.C.A. and I hope to see its continued development in the years to come.

Opposite: Prince Philip examining the dinghy with George Vince (on his left).

Fairthorne Manor *At the bottom of the picture is believed to be the old Roman road which goes into the footpath and fords the river.*

Botleigh Grange

Botleigh Grange was built as a country house during the 16th century. It is said that around this period Oliver Cromwell came to stay. The estate at this time consisted of over 100 acres which contained a large freshwater lake, with a small but beautiful weir, where it overflowed as a cascade into a small lake on its way to the sea.

Thomas Hellyer Foord, a shipbuilder and contractor of Rochester, purchased the 100-acre estate in 1868. He was responsible for the addition of a tower over the porch which housed a clock with Westminster Chimes, by Buggins of Clerkenwell. The internal decorations were carried out by one of the family's own decorators, the principle additions being the oak panelled walls and a unique ornamental ceiling. The carved mantlepiece depicting acorns, may have been a reminder of the family business carried out at Acorn Wharf. Mr. Foord being fond of animals established a herd of 200 deer on the estate. Thomas Hellyer Foord died at the age of 93 in 1917. Near the top of St. John's Road you will see Foord Road named after him.

The Grange was eventually sold in lots in 1923 leaving the mansion with only 25 acres of gardens and lakes. It was converted into a private hotel in 1932 and continued as such until the Plumpton family purchased it in 1949. They acquired a full licence to run the Botleigh Grange Hotel as a licensed country house hotel. There are a variety of rooms: the Grange Rooms, the Cromwell Rooms and the Queen Mary and Queen Elizabeth four-poster bedrooms. A magnificent dining room, described as the most attractive in Hampshire, was added in 1991. There are conference rooms with high ceilings and windows overlooking the gardens and lakes.

Enquiries to the Botleigh Grange Hotel, Grange Road, Hedge End, Southampton SO3 2GA or telephone (0489) 788535.

Botley Park Hotel and Country Club

Among many new developments in the Hedge End area is the Botley Park Hotel and Country Club.

Described as an exciting new hotel and country club, it is set in its own landscaped parkland which imaginatively combines all the qualities of a luxury hotel together with the attractions of one of the finest leisure complexes in the region. The hotel is a luxury retreat for a perfect relaxing break with superb appointments for a business venue, meetings, conferences and banqueting.

Members of the Botley Park Golf and Leisure Club as well as hotel guests will have exclusive access to one of the most magnificently equipped leisure clubs in the area.

In addition to the indoor swimming pool, there is tennis and squash, petanque, croquet, putting, exercise and aerobics suite, snooker, spa pool, sauna, steam room, solarium and, of course, golf.

Functions rooms are available for parties up to 250 people with projectors, screens, video, PA systems, lighting, etc. There is a conference manager on hand to help you design a successful event.

Enquiries to: Botley Park Hotel and Country Club, Winchester Road, Boorley Green, Botley, Hants. SO3 2UA or telephone (0489) 780888.

Back to Hedge End . . .

Twinning
Comines — Hedge End

Comines is a town of 11,300 people situated on the French/Belgian border. The border is actually the River Lys which runs through the middle of Comines. The bridge over the river does not look like a border between two countries although on one side is Comines, Belgium while on the other Comines, France. From Calais, Comines can be reached in one-and-a-half hours but this will become three-quarters of an hour with the opening of the new motorway due to be finished this year (1992). For the moment the route takes the Dunkirk road and heads towards Lille which is 19km from Comines.

Comines is a lovely town with an impressive square, overlooked by the Town Hall with an ornate steeple and clock. Soon it will become Comines Europe and the Mayors of the two towns (French and Belgian) have, since 1989, drawn up a plan for the development of the area — as it was vital to keep the north-western area of France active following the closure of the pits. Comines has 40 acres in France and 100 acres in Belgium for development — prime land which is green belt type land approximately one-third cheaper than in England. There will soon be four new motorways to this area and the waterway, the River Lys, is being dredged to take up to 3,000-tonne vessels within the next five years. Currently it can take 400-tonne vessels.

British companies are being encouraged to set up business in the area — already Reckitts Colman have established a company Reckitts Couleur, manufacturing blue plasticware, and the concessions and monetary advantages are designed to encourage industrial development.

Comines has had some difficulty with the constitution of its Twinning Association. Unlike us they are subject to the various ramifications of corporate law, complicated by the fact that they operate in two countries.

Some Dates of Interest

1956 Hedge End Branch of the Women's Institute was formed.
1958 The RSPCA Animal Welfare Centre was established.
1960 The Ladies' Life Boat Guild was formed.
1962 On April 28 the Village Hall was opened. A few years later it was extended to provide a small hall for the library.
1971 Opening of the tennis courts on the playing fields.
1972 Scout and Guide headquarters were opened in Allen Road.
1974 Under local government re-organisation on April 1, Hedge End was transferred from Winchester Rural District Council to Eastleigh Borough Council.
1976 The Recreation Centre for the Retired (Day Centre) was opened.
1978 The Hedge End section of the M27 was opened.
1978 On March 29 H.R.H. Princess Margaret opened the Queen Elizabeth II Silver Jubilee Activity Centre for the Disabled.
1990 May — Opening of the new Hedge End Railway Station.

The Catherine Wheel

At a meeting of what was known as The Catherine Wheel Committee on Wednesday, 4th December 1963, Dr. A. S. Pern gave his winding-up speech.

The Committee was formed on 8th September 1903 with the following members, Rev. G. E. C. Osborne, Mrs. Osborne, Lady Jenkyns, Rev. A. Markby and Messrs. A. Jenkyns, Beckett-Powell, J. Matthews, A. Parker and W. Lewry. They met to attempt to continue the work of Canon Lee of Botley and Mrs. Lee who with her ladies ran it as a 'Temperance Establishment'. Quite a change from its origins as one of Botley's 13 public houses. The Committee then appointed a Manager to run it as a Temperance Hotel and Coffee House.

During the Second World War the premises were kept in good use accommodating troops and evacuees. The Committee also ran the Old Age Pensioners' Association and provided meeting rooms for the members.

When the Committee decided to sell the business it was also decided that the purchasers would have to be Botley people. Mrs. R. Taylor had spent all her life in Botley and her husband almost all his life so they were able to purchase the business.

Today the Catherine Wheel is owned by Derek Fagg and is run as a Bakers and Confectioners with a reputation extending well beyond the Parish of Botley. In the entrance to the shop you can see an exposed panel of the original walls built with wattle and daub.

Opposite: Interior of the Catherine Wheel today.

The choir of St. John's Church, Hedge End in the 1970s

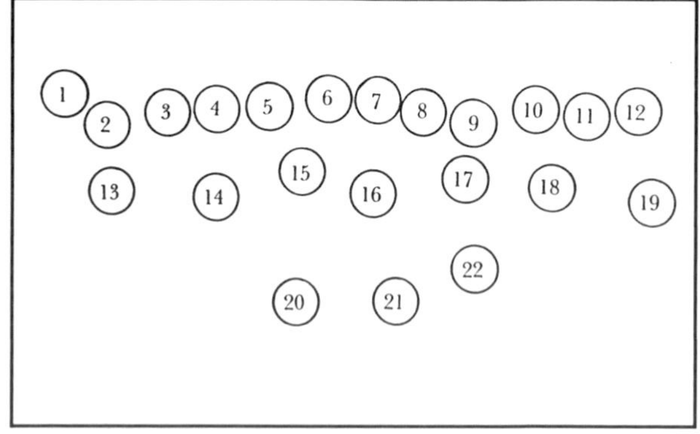

1.
2.
3. Seldon
4. Peter Spencer
5. Victor Terry
6. Rev. Heard
7. Roy Kilford
8. Kenneth Watts
9.
10. Terrence Gleed
11. Richard Wharmby
12. David Ansell
13. Adrian Boggust
14.
15.
16.
17. Ian Watts
18. Miller
19.
20.
21.
22.

Do you know the missing names?

Acknowledgements

Before we end — and to make sure we do not forget, let's do it now — we must thank a large number of people for their help in so many ways in connection with this book. They include:

Cllr. Peter Madsen, Mayor of Eastleigh

Frank Mortimer

Dr. Robin Marsh

Eastleigh Borough Council

Malcolm Butler

Joyce B. Blyth

Mrs. Edmunds, Hedge End W.I.

Len Shelton, Eastleigh Borough Council

Mr. B. J. Sullivan, Goring by Sea

Mrs. Greta Hindmarsh

Manor Farm Museum

Mrs. Delia Pugh, Botley Primary School

Martin McLellan, Grange Aviaries

George Vince

Botleigh Grange

Botley Park Hotel and Country Club

Mrs. Beryl Hollinrake

Roger Vane

Gary Chase

Mrs. Margaret Lavery of Botley

Mrs. C. King of Botley

Mr. Robert Nimmo

Mrs. Rosemary Foot (Chairlady of the Wildern Society)

The Misses Maffey of Botley

Rev. Spencer Underhill

Miss Daphne Macnoe and Mrs. Maureen Badnell of Hedge End W.I.

Epilogue

Since the Domesday Book these villages have seen massive changes.

Amazingly in not far short of 1,000 years the most dramatic and extensive changes have taken place in the last decade.

The green fields of Hedge End which I knew when I first came here are lost under the development which brought Marks and Spencer, Sainsbury, Halfords, Courts, Texas, Great Mills, Power, Furnitureland, McDonalds with its drive through (albeit a tight squeeze), the industrial parks and plans for more to come. How long will it be before Hedge End and Botley find themselves at the centre of a great Solent City? — where once the dinosaur roamed the delta of the mighty Solent River.

Bill Lyon